THE STORY OF JUNE:
A LOON CHICK IN MAINE

by Roger L. Stevens, Jr.

First Edition

Published by Maine Focus Photography
P.O. Box 398
Lincoln, Maine 04457

Copyright 2014 by Maine Focus Photography

If you have any questions or comments about this book, you can contact Roger L. Stevens, Jr at:
Maine Focus Photography
P.O. Box 398
Lincoln, Maine 04457
1-877-794-1928
mefocus@myfairpoint.net
www.mainefocusphotography.biz

Proudly Manufactured in the U.S.A. by:
J.S. McCarthy Printers
15 Darin Drive
Augusta, Maine 04330

ISBN 978-0-578-14994-3

For information about custom editions, special sales, and retail orders, please contact Maine Focus Photography.

Living in Lincoln, Maine, an area that boasts 13 lakes and ponds, I have had the privilege of watching and filming these amazing birds, the Common Loons, over many years. What I have observed is a creature that was designed to "fly" underwater, catch fish and other food with ease, and love and care for its chicks with a tenderness and attentiveness that is inspirational.

I hope this book teaches you more about this beautiful, mysterious bird, and maybe awakens the memory of the first time you were fortunate enough to see a loon or hear its lovely call.

Sincerely,

Roger L. Stevens, Jr.

Roger L. Stevens, Jr.
Maine Focus Photography

Roger L. Stevens

It was early spring in Maine as the lakes were slowly breaking free of the ice that had covered them over the winter. The loons were returning from their winter homes in the open saltwater of the Atlantic Ocean to the places where they were born. Their calls sounded like someone yodeling in the sky.

Each loon swam around the lakes and ponds where he or she had
lived the year before, calling for the mates whom they had chosen for life.
Soon they heard the unique cries that were so familiar to them.

One pair of loons finally found each other in the midst of floating ice, happy to be together again on the lake they knew so well.

After dancing and stretching, their thoughts turned to nest-building and the hope of producing another loon chick that would call this place, Silver Lake, its home.

They searched for the old nesting site they had chosen before, close to the water yet hidden enough to keep the eggs safe from predators like raccoons and mink. Soon they found it.

They restored the old nest with new
moss and tiny sticks. The mother
loon laid a single mottled egg, and
the process of guarding the egg and always keeping it a comfortable temperature began.

The loons sat and sat through day and night, warm days and cold ones, relieving each other long enough for a stretch and a bite of fish.

After 29 days of both parent loons turning the egg, warming the egg, cooling the egg, and protecting the egg, it started to slowly crack open.

The mother loon could hear the faint cries of the little chick through the crack in the egg that sat beneath her.

She let out a low, hooting cry to let the father loon know it was time.
Time to greet another loon chick into the world!

So on that day in late June, a new loon chick sat on the edge of her nest beside Silver Lake, and I called her June the Loon.

Resting briefly to recover her
strength, June tottered
toward the water and into the
protection of her waiting father.

With a soft hoot, he welcomed her into the watery world that she would call home, leaving it only to sit upon a nest of her own some day.

Father Loon brought June her first meal,
a sunfish so big that June couldn't begin to eat it!

Mother Loon brought her a chewed-up piece of a fish that was more June-sized.

And then the loon parents went for a paddle with June, proudly showing her off to the rest of Silver Lake. June's small feet paddled and paddled to keep up!

After a while, June's legs grew tired from all that paddling and she began to get sleepy.

With a lot of splashing and a lift from her mother's wing,
June climbed up onto the warm, dry back of her parent.

Safe atop her mother, June stretched her long legs and feet out behind her

and snuggled up close to her parent's neck, knowing she was
sitting in the safest place for a loon chick on all of Silver Lake.

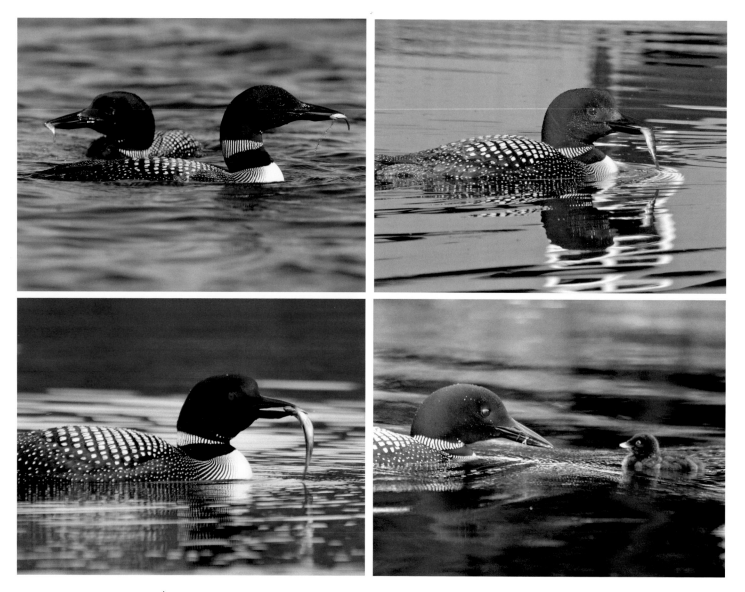

So June's parents spent most of their days catching food for her, with offerings of minnows and crayfish

which June hungrily and happily accepted!

Soon her parents dropped their catches so that June had
to put her head underwater to retrieve them

and that is how June learned to dive and fish for herself.

And the diving lessons were VERY important the day the hungry eagle tried to catch a loon chick for his meal.

As the eagle's shadow passed by, June's mother yelled an alarm hoot, then signaled for June to dive.

June's father, fishing at the other end of the lake, heard the mother's calls and flew back as fast as he could.

He landed and began to splash water all about, dancing and crying to confuse the eagle while June and her mother slid quietly to safety under a dock on the opposite shoreline.

After luring the eagle to the far shore of the lake, Father Loon dove deeply and swam swiftly underwater. Surfacing on the other shore with June and her mother, he knew the danger had passed, *this* time.

The summer continued with June growing in size
and learning what it was like to be a loon.

When Father Loon stretched his wings, June would stretch HER wings

and when Mother Loon would preen her feathers, June would preen HER feathers!

But she still liked climbing on her parents' backs best of all

because whether you are a loon chick or a little child,
you are NEVER too big for a good snuggle.

The summer passed quickly and thanks to her parents' fishing skills,
June the loon chick grew, and grew, and GREW!

Cool nights signaled the arrival of fall and the mature loons gathered
in groups to begin their migration to the ocean waters that never freeze,
where they could swim and catch food all winter long.

By now, June had learned how to fish for herself and how to dive from danger. She had also practiced flapping her wings to cross the lake but like all other adolescent loons, she was still unable to fly. It would be a few more weeks until her flight feathers appeared.

She knew instinctively that her parents were preparing to join the other adults in their journey to the ocean. Although she knew she could live by herself, she was a little afraid and lonesome.

June cried a low, keening call as she rubbed against her mother's neck. It was almost as if she was asking her to stay. June had grown accustomed to having her parents around for safety and comfort.

But her mother knew that June had grown into a strong, young loon and with a few low hoots, assured June that everything would be fine. "Follow your instincts, and follow the rivers south as soon as you can fly. You will find us at the ocean," she seemed to say.

And so at daybreak the very next day, the parent loons of Silver Lake gathered together. After saying farewell to their chicks, one by one they flew off in the direction of the ocean.

June watched her parents fly away, and she flapped her wings
as if to bid them a safe journey. In a few weeks, when her flight feathers were
ready, she would join the other adolescent loons of the lake and fly south, too.

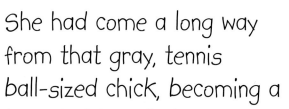

She had come a long way from that gray, tennis ball-sized chick, becoming a beautiful juvenile loon in three short months. She could dive, hold her breath for a long time, and catch all the fish she needed. She was aware of danger from the sky and knew how to escape it. She had all the skills she needed to live on her own.

June could hardly wait to fly south for the winter with rest of the young loons from Silver Lake, and to see her parents again. She knew that the lake would be there to welcome her home after it shed its coat of ice the next spring. And THAT would be ANOTHER adventure for June the Loon!

This book is dedicated to my mother, Carolyn, who oohed and aahed over my fir[st] attempts to photograph loons over 40 years ago, when they were just black and white dots on a gray background. Thank you for supporting me in my photographic journey, and for the many years we spent as a family at our camp on Long Pond enjoying these beautiful creatures.

And to three special "chicks", Dana, Britt, and Chance, who love the Grand State of Maine, summers at camp, loons and all things wild. Thank you for fishing trips, circus shows, and singalongs, especially our signature song. "Take it away!" Love you all.